To: Betsy

From: Mary Edna
+
Florence

August 4, 1994

WITH
FRIENDS

written and illustrated
by
Susan Squellati Florence

The C.R. Gibson Company, Norwalk, Ct. 06856

If there is one ingredient
which adds warmth
and love to our lives...
it is friendship.

If there is one relationship
to help us through
all the others...
it is friendship.

Friends surround us
with the beauty
of their caring.

With friends
we can
share

what we see,
what we feel,
what we love.

Friends help us
with our problems
because they listen.

And as they listen
we begin to hear
the language
of our own hearts.

With friends
we can walk along
the remembered paths
of our lives
and completely share
our experiences.

With friends
we can work the soil
of forgotten dreams
that need to be
tended and nurtured
once again.

With friends
we can plant
the seeds
of our heart's
new dreams.

We can always
return to a friend
like going back
to a special place...
and find the same
warm feeling,
unchanged by time
or distance.

Life gives us friends
so we can share
the precious times
and memorable moments

of being children,
and teenagers,
and adults,
and parents,
and grandparents.

Life gives us friends
so we can share
the growing up...
and the growing old.

With friends
we have a place to go
to be accepted
and understood.

Together
we can laugh,
together
we can cry...

our thoughts
are heard,
our feelings
are held
in the heart
of a friend.

32

With friends
our lives are more full,
more rich,
more open ...
beautiful
and blessed.